SIXTY YEARS OF POETRY FROM THE HEARTLAND

FRITZ FUHS

DEDICATION

To My
Incredible Family

INTRODUCTION

Many years ago I attended Iowa State Teachers College with an English major. It is now called the University of Northern Iowa. Consequently, during the last forty years or more, I have pretended that I am a poet. As you read this booklet, I deeply appreciate your encouraging my fantasy.

CONTENTS

CHAPTER I - MY FIRST POEM

I enlisted in the Air Force when I was twenty-one, during the Korean Conflict. My squadron was included in a military maneuver that took place in the barren northwest part of Texas. In trying to explain to my family what a unique experience it turned out to be, I wrote my very first poem.

THE MANEUVER

Me? I joined the Air Force.
They promised a fine career.
And everything went just as planned
For a little over a year.

And then I finally made the grade.
My tech school days were done.
But had I known what they had in store,
I'd gone AWOL on the run.

I'll have to admit, as I reminisce,
That it didn't seem I'd been cursed,
When they gave me orders for the Sunny South
To join the 131st.

Well, I wasn't there any more than a week
When I first got word of my fate;
Somebody volunteered the whole damned outfit
For a maneuver in the Lone Star State.

Of course, I was one of the lucky ones;
They made a driver out of me.
But I'd rather have ridden the Old Gray Mare
Than driven that rattling, old P.C.

"Oh beautiful, beautiful Texas,
The most beautiful land that I know."
You can be sure the man that wrote those words
Never saw our campsite in sheep shit row.

You know, I think the man that picked that site
Must have had his head in his proverbial ass,
Because in two months time in the dusty place
I never saw a drop of water, or a blade of grass.

And just as the recruiting officer said,
"There is a skill field for every man to explore."
Believe me, I discovered all there was to learn
About a shit-hole, eight, by six, by four.

But then we finally got to going,
And a radio mechanic was much in demand.
I got so I could fix a radio
Without even lifting a hand.

They'd phone me up in a desperate voice
As if all hope were gone.
Then with profound wisdom I'd give my reply,
"How about turning the damned thing on."

But finally they set the date to come home,
And the General addressed us with, "Well done men."
And just for a moment I forgot where I was,
And felt proud to be in the Air Force again.

Wow! I'll never forget the trip home.
I was helping old Bob drive a van.
It was designed to go 50, it would do 60,
But we were doing 70 when we passed the lead man.

They say the paratroopers have it rough.
That very few men make the grade.
But after this, you know what? I'm going to transfer.
I'm convinced those guys got it made.

CHAPTER II - THE SEASONS

Growing up on an Iowa farm, I was always intrigued by the four seasons. I looked forward to and enjoyed each one for its special uniqueness.

SPRING

Spring is frogs
 And clean, cool water;
  Flowers that can't be bought or sold,
   And buds that only birds behold.

Spring is winter in perspective;
 Summertime without its sweat,
  And autumn color passing lightly,
   Asking where
    We might have met.

Spring is babies
 Bright and babbling;
  Youth with all its pulsing power.
   And for young and old alike
    It seems to be the loving hour.

Spring is sadness, Spring is joy;
 Mother Nature's favorite toy;
  Frogs and colors,
   Love and babies.
    Springtime is a million maybes.

SUMMER

Lying on the grass and looking at the clouds
Swinging on a grapevine and dropping in the water
Riding my bike along the Mississippi River
Waiting for a catfish to bite on my worm
Pitching my tent in the old camp ground
Singing round the campfire pit
Picking and podding the new green peas
Hiking with my friend on the Old Hickory Trail
Taking my grandchildren to the zoo
Cutting and arranging a bouquet of flowers
Watching my kids play Dad's Club softball
Cooking steak on the back yard grill
Running around barefoot all day long
Planning a picnic at Wildcat Den
Taking trips to brand new places
Walking in the rain without an umbrella
Building sand castles on the beach
Slipping down the slides at the water park
Attending the annual family reunion
Going to the Scott County Fair
Eating hot dogs at the baseball game

FALL

When the leaves begin to turn
And the woods explode with color,
I feel as though an artist,
An incredibly talented artist,

With a monumental brush,
And an infinite choice of paint,
Has come for a brief visit,
To show us what life could be like,

If we let our imagination
Team up with our elation,
And broaden our expectation,
We would reach the realization
That life is a sensation
Comparable to any artist's dream.

Fall is like a summary
Of the entire year,
When we gather all together
Every smile and every tear.

There's a little bit of summer,
And a little bit of spring,
And a warning of the winter
That the autumn breezes bring.

There's a sadness in the summary
Of the year that has just passed,
But the explosion of its color
Is the memory that will last.

WINTER

Old Man Winter roared in last night,
When I was fast asleep.
He must have had a rendezvous
He felt he had to keep,

With the wild, wild wind,
And the silent snow
That filled my yard,
And the field below

With waist-high drifts,
And big round mounds
Of pure, white snow,
And whistling sounds.

I don't know where he comes from,
But it must be a pretty place,
With white-flocked trees,
And bright-red birds,
And a snowman's funny face.

Some people long for springtime
With its flowers and new-green look.
Some people tell you summertime
Is like living in a storybook.

Some people love the autumn leaves
That fall all around the place,
But I still prefer the wintertime
That makes my old blood race.

CHAPTER III – PLANTS

My maternal grandfather was an old English gardener. From him I learned the joy of growing plants.

CLIVIA

Each year before the tulips bloom
I go to the Park's big greenhouse room,
And see the Clivia, orange and all.
I wish they bloomed from Spring to Fall.

Their burst of color beyond a dream
Is one of the flowers that seem
To dominate the space they take,
And without a doubt will always make
A person do a double take.
They seem unreal as a birthday cake.

Orange is one of my favorite colors,
And there is no orange as fair
As the clivia blossom that
Fills the greenhouse with its beauty so rare.

Clivia, Clivia how do you dare
To come back each spring and have your affair
With each soul that doesn't seem aware
That your blossom has an eternal air.

A CORN STORY

From a little yellow kernel
Comes Iowa's claim to fame.
The Indians called it maize,
Back when the Pilgrims came.

We plant our corn in early Spring,
As soon as the soil is right.
It grows so fast, and is so green,
A cornfield is a wondrous sight.

Corn loves our hot and humid Summer.
It seldom fails to grow.
It also loves our deep, black soil,
That supports it row on row.

Come July it starts to bloom.
The blossom is its tassel.
Green soldiers marching all around
The barn; the Iowa Castle.

To produce our hybrid seed corn
Some tassels must be banned,
So that only special pollen
Will meet the golden strand.

Then comes the cool, crisp days of Fall.
Ears hanging long on stalks so tall
Must be picked; the work begins.
The corn is stored in metal bins.

A corn picker is a huge machine
That gathers ears, and shells them too,
From browning stalks, dead from the frost.
But strong enough to still stand true.

The golden kernels fill the bins.
The stalks are baled for bedding.
The fields are once more bare and cold.
The hills are free for sledding.

Through the winter the rich soil rests,
And dreams of its former glory,
But knows that come the Springtime
There will be a new corn story.

A WEED

How does it feel
To be a weed?
To forever know
You can't succeed

No matter how hard
You try to please,
Even though you know
You also lure the bees.

Even though you know
You have beauty too.
But you also know that
No matter what you do

You happen not to be
In the proper place.
So being a weed
Is what you face.

It really isn't fair
You know
To brand one a weed
Just because they grow

In a place where they
Appear to be different from
The ones who think they're
In the know.

A weed has the right
To grow and bloom
Wherever it happens
To find sufficient room.

It doesn't need to
Match the ones around.
It has its own life.
It deserves its own ground.

CHAPTER IV - DAVENPORT

I've lived in Davenport a long time. It's been a wonderful place to work and raise our family. It has many unique facets that make it a special place.

VANDERVEER

I went to the park on a sweet summer day,
And slowly I strolled down the Grand Allee.
It was VanderVeer magic that touched my heart.
The special park aura was the very best part.

The fabulous fountain
Like a bubbling mountain
Was a wondrous sight.
You must come and see its colors at night.

I could hear the breeze
As it kissed the green trees,
And played little jokes
On the stately old oaks.

I saw the ducks splash a tune
On the lovely lagoon.
I saw the bronze children play
In their own silent way.

I know I could smell the rose garden hues
Midst the yellows and reds and even some blues.
And the pergola framed in its own special way
The wedding that played on that magical day.

I hope no one lets their summer pass by
Without a VanderVeer visit like I
Strolled in the park on that sweet summer day
Down the beautiful, magical Grand Allee.

WE LOVE OUR SKATE PARK

In a world of the couch potato
And the computer geek,
We ride the air to seek
The world upside down;
A feeling royal and round.
We strain to capture
The weightless rapture
That comes from flying
With no wings.
Oh, the high it brings
To the ones with the guts
To fall on their butts,
And jump up again
To ride the rim.
And, finally, it isn't a sin
For the her or the him
To love the thrill
Of the dip and the hill
That propels them along
Like an endless, sweet song.
It gives them hope
For something better than dope.
It helps them cope
When life tightens the rope
That keeps them down
When they want to clown,

And forget the frown
From the old one around
Who says, "Stay on the ground!"

CREDIT ISLAND

Long before the white man came,
Indians roamed this Midwest plain.
They paddled down the rivers blue,
And I'm sure they slept on this island too.

They visited the Credit Island site
When they wanted to rest and have a bite.
I'm sure they enjoyed this special place
As much as I do when I race.

We often go and walk the trail,
And watch the river boaters sail.
The wildlife is a wondrous sight,
As they scurry through the lacy light.

The egrets with their snow-white plume
Are feeding in the old lagoon.
The big blue herons fly slowly by.
They remind me of a silent sigh.

The long-necked stately Canada geese
Feed in gaggles on the wild, wet grass.
The mallard ducks, a loving pair,
Wander like a moonstruck lad and lass.

Credit Island is a place to walk and play,
And dream about a former day.
May it always remain our island paradise
Where we can enjoy nature so wild and wise.

SKYWALK

From Second Street to the flowing river,
From the heart of town, a glowing sliver
That takes me through the sky.
We're really up so high
That we can see from the eastern bridge
To the city's western ridge.

Or if it's in the evening glow,
We can watch the sunset slow.
Or if it's early morning,
We watch the same sun borning.

I love to look down on our city
Like the birds that fly so high.
Each time I walk the shiny path
I look down in rapture and sigh.

I no longer envy the eagles
That fill our sky in the winter time,
Because I can now also
Soar over our town just anytime.

THE BIG SCREEN

I went to see the movie
On the great big screen;
I had no idea how really big.
It was the biggest I'd ever seen.

I put on the funny glasses.
I didn't really know why.
I didn't realize the picture
Would end up so very nigh.

I felt I was part of the action
In every scary scene.
I experienced that show
In every single gene.

If I were looking at a spider,
It was crawling on my gown.
If I were floating down a river,
I knew I was going to drown.

If I were flying in an airplane,
We barely missed the mountains.
If I were on the streets of Rome,
I could barely duck the fountains.

Actually, I am now a big screen fan.
I intend to go again as soon as I can.

THE MISSISSIPPI RIVER

A playground, a scene,
A valuable source;
Our abundant river
Silently runs its course.

Called The Father Of Waters,
So majestic and great,
It's always been here,
From the earliest date.

It's a highway for barges,
With its buoys and its locks.
It's the fishermen's home,
For their boats and their docks.

It's the sail boater's dream
On any one of its lakes.
It's a home for the mallards,
Both the hens and the drakes.

It's a beautiful river
When kissed by the sun.
Of all the great rivers,
It's the greatest one.

WILDCAT DEN STATE PARK

Fifteen miles down the river
Is a very small price to pay
For the thrill of walking the trails
At the park on a bright summer's day.

If you walk the trail in early April,
You'll see the hepatica bloom.
In May the Dutchman's breeches
Will fill the woodland room.

Underneath the sandstone bluffs
Steamboat rock will loom quite high,
And further along the winding trail
The devil's Punchbowl will make you sigh.

Be sure to stop at the Pine Creek Mill,
Built in eighteen thirty-eight.
It's been carefully restored
By a hard-working group who rate
Very high on the volunteer scale,
Carefully rebuilding with hammer and nail.

As the water rushes over the dam,
And spills into the pond below,
Children might be splashing around
As the Pine Creek waters flow.

Or maybe you would like to camp,
And spend a day or two.
If you did, you'd long remember
Your Wildcat rendezvous.

OUR EAGLES

I love to watch the eagles fly.
They seem to punctuate the sky.
They soar with awesome, silent grace
As they scrutinize our tiny place.

What is it like
To fly so high;
To live above
Both you and I?

In winter time
They come to feed
On tasty fish.
It's quite a deed
As they eye on high

The swimming fish,
And diving down
Catch on the fly.

If I could be something other than me,
If I could play another role,
I'd choose to be a great big bird;
An eagle with a human soul.

THE FIGGE ART MUSEUM

Many call it a huge glass box;
Only dessert for the elite.
When actually it's bread and butter for anyone
Willing to take the time to visit our local treasure.

The rolling hills of Iowa
When viewed through the eyes of Grant Wood,
Are seen for what they really are;
The fertile breadbaskets of the world.

The uneducated, poor people of Haiti
Become colorful jugglers of joy,
When viewed through the eyes
Of their talented, native artists.

Visiting collections from around the country
Allow us an expanding understanding
Of the most diverse cultural
Treasures the world has ever seen.

Yes, we spent millions of dollars
On a huge glass box
That illuminates centuries of insight
Glowing in the artwork of incredible interpreters.

CHAPTER V - NATURE

Spending my life in the Midwest has fueled my love of nature, and the beauty of the countryside in general.

IOWA
(WITH APOLOGIES TO ROBERT BROWNING)

Oh, to be in Iowa
Now that April's there,
And whoever wakes in Iowa
Sees, some morning, unaware,
That the bloodroot blooms at Wildcat Den,
And the mushrooms grow in the secret glen,
While the robin sings on the orchard bough
In Iowa—now!

SHELTERED

He walked in a sheltered forest,
Wondered at the shadows,
And marveled at the strength of the
Trees that kept the storm from him.

But he longed for a glimpse of the sun,
And for the feel of the wind in his face.
So slowly, very slowly, he fought
His way out of the shadows;
Resolved to leave the forest forever behind.

He couldn't bear the sun in its
Full glory, so he built a house.
The wind made his body raw
Until he clothed himself.
And longing for a shadow he wondered at his own.

He walks in a sheltered forest

THE WIND

There are stars in the sky
That can see the living lie.
There are birds in the blue
That sometimes scream.

There are fish in the sea
That know of you and me,
Because the wind plays
The fool in our dream.

STONE WALLS

I love stone walls.
I don't know why.
They seem so strong
When I walk by.

I feel so safe.
They provide protection;
They keep things out.
They hold a section

Of the earth,
In a very special way.
They're like strong arms
Hugging the whole long day.

A flower planted by
A stone wall,
Will smile and grow
Beautiful and tall.

Or maybe an ivy
Will grow right out of the stack,
Sending its roots
Back into a cool, damp crack.

A courtyard surrounded
By a tall stone wall
Becomes a nature room
That seems to call

Me from whatever
I might be doing,
Like a lover
Calling and wooing,

Telling me to
Leave the busy outside teem,
And come into the special world
Where I could rest and dream.

If only my life
Was surrounded
By a courtyard wall,
I'm sure I would have
No worries at all.

SUNRISE

Dawn; a new day,
After the sleepy night,
A blank slate
On which to write.

We must welcome
What comes our way,
Not knowing if good or bad.
Not knowing if happy or sad.

Choices we hourly make.
Numerous options arrive.
We know not which to take,
But we are forced to dive

One way or another
Into the murky deep,
Hoping to meet a brother
Who will help us keep

Our balance, and
The amazing air
That keeps our body
Alive as we dare

To face another day,
Not knowing if we will
See the sunset that
Says we've had our fill.

RABBITS

A bunny is a furry bit;
A hopping, energetic guy.
He never threatens anyone.
I'm sure he wouldn't hurt a fly.

He seems to be a vegan,
Preferring tender clover.
He likes to play with all his friends.
They say he's quite a lover.

I wish that all of humankind
Were more like this friendly one.
We'd never lie, or cheat, or fight,
And life would be more fun.

OUR WALK

We took a walk one day
Along a winding, woodland way.
The sun was shining on the clay
Of the path we chose that day.

We didn't talk,
Because when you walk
There is no need to say aloud
What one feels floating on a cloud.

Walking, one feels the world,
And knows it's completely round.
Each step further proves the truth
That can only be found

By caressing the earth
With the feet we've been given.
And the farther we walk
The more we'll be driven

To discover the secrets
That lie in the soil.
If we come close enough
To make it a Royal

Road instead of a path,
We'll find the release
That a walk can give
Is a powerful peace.

WATERFALLS

I love the falling waters.
I love the mist, the rainbow.
I love the lilting laughter
As they kiss the rocks below.

I'd love to spend eternity
In a lovely perfect pool,
Where the fun-filled falling waters
Would massage and keep me cool.

SNOW

I remember drifts as high as mountains,
And hillsides daring my sled and me.
I remember tunnels we dug to hide in,
And forts where we crawled on hand and knee.

The white, and whispering, whistling snow
Would create a whitewashed, whirlwind sight,
Where we played all day with frozen toes,
And still excited, dreamed all night.

Then, when the weather finally mellowed ,
And the snow would pack like a cotton ball,
We'd build the biggest snowman ever,
Three balls high, and six feet tall.

Sometimes a cold snap would freeze the snow,
And we could walk on top the mounds.
That's when we'd sit on big scoop shovels,
And go down the hill like a pack of hounds.

Many people curse the snow,
And see it as an awful blight.
I only remember with childhood awe
Of a whispering, whistling, whirlwind sight.

CHAPTER VI - NONSENSE

Some things should not be taken seriously. We call them nonsense, and yet they project a special kind of truth.

CLOTHES

We wear clothes for many reasons;
Primarily to protect our skin.
But when it's warm and sunny,
We think no clothes a sin.

It feels so good to skinny dip.
I've tried it and I know.
Or when the weather's nice and warm
I'll tell you how I'd like to go.

I'd like to run around all bare.
I'd like to wear no clothes at all.
So people see me as God does.
Why should that scene appall?

I'm not ashamed of my naked self.
It's what God gave my soul.
It's a body I'm supposed to care for.
It's all I have to play my role.

They say that clothes can make the man.
I say that clothes oft times portray
A false and wrong impression,
And the real man they betray.

I think if every one of us
Was bound to appear quite nude,
We'd care more for our body,
And might even be less rude.

THE REAL WORLD

It's rocks down below,
And clouds up above.
It's spending some time,
With the people you love.

It's singing and laughing,
And working long hours.
It's trees and mountains,
And beautiful flowers.

It's wishing for millions,
And working for nickels.
It's dreaming of steak,
And settling for pickles

It's flying an airplane,
And driving a car.
It's climbing a mountain,
And running too far.

It's a daily rendezvous
With the sun and the moon.
And when it's all over
Dying too soon.

BONGO

Burning, bungling beetles
Bellow, bellow, bellow.

Brawny, brown bugs
Bitter, bitter, bitter.

Bloody, blood blotters
Bubble, bubble, bubble.

Bulging, barracuda bellies
Beat, beat, beat.

CLIMBING

Some people call life a stream,
Which we continually float down.
Some people call life a battle;
Something they face with a frown.

Some people call life a journey,
Where we travel on different roads.
Some days we travel lightly.
Other days we carry heavy loads.

I believe life is a mountain;
A mountain of infinite size,
Where we climb each day of our life,
And as long as we climb we arise.

Some days we think the climb is tough.
Some days the terrain is mighty rough.
Some days the sun is shining bright,
Especially on days we choose the right.
Some days the clouds are very dark,
And our climb seems to have lost its spark.

But if we keep on climbing
No matter how hard it seems,
We will have a happy life,
And realize our most precious dreams.

HOW TO EAT A GOOSEBERRY

First you tail it.
Then you stem it.
Then you suck it for an hour.

So when you crunch it,
And you eat it,
Then it won't be quite so sour.

LICE IN PERSPECTIVE

No one ever died
From lice in the hair.
In fact there are times
We don't know they're there.

No one ever gets sick
From these little mites.
They don't even seem
To violate our rights.

And yet when we found them
Such panic resulted,
If I were the lice
I'd be quite insulted.

BACK SEAT

I was assigned the back seat
In a six-passenger van.
I didn't realize I would feel like
A sardine in a very small can.

I couldn't stretch my legs.
I couldn't recline my seat.
After two or three hours,
I knew I was really beat.

Finally we stopped to rest.
I couldn't wait for him to park.
The only trouble was
I was too cramped to disembark.

The only thing worse than getting out
Was trying to get back in.
I tried it going backwards; I nearly broke my shin.
I knew it was a contest I was never going to win.

If I ever take another trip
In a six-passenger car,
I'm going to spend my packing time
In a very generous bar.

THINGS

Things are a burden
From which I'll divest.
I'll burn all my toys,
And throw away all the rest.

I have many things
I picked on the way.
I knew I would want
To enjoy them some day.

But things have a way
Of holding me down.
What hair I still have
Does not need a crown.

Things tend to surround me
Now that I'm old.
They no longer amuse me.
They leave me so cold.

I become claustrophobic
As though I may drown
In the myriad of memories
They seem to surround.

I don't need a car
Long as I can still walk.
I don't need a mike
To enhance my small talk.

I don't need some wine
To tickle my tongue.
Cool, clear water
Will help keep me young.

I don't need the ring
Round my finger no more
To remind of the love
That still lives in my core.

I don't need a tux
To adorn my old flesh.
I love my old wrinkles,
And I now only wish
I could run about naked
And swim like a fish.

It's time to enjoy
My life as God gave it.
No more will I grasp
And decide then to save it.

I need a sunrise to start my new day.
I need a garden in which I can play.
I need a bed to nurture my dream.
It could be the sod by a swift, sunlit stream.

I need a friend
To unburden my soul.
The games that we play
Will help keep me whole.

I only need love
To make me feel free.
I only need you
If you'll still cling to me.
Until we both leave
All this world and these things
That we'll no longer need
When the golden bell rings

I'M IN HIGH SCHOOL NOW

I'm in high school now,
And I've got the world by its tailpipe.
Soon as I get some asbestos gloves
I'm going to swing it till it's red-ripe,

And then sudden-like let go,
And watch it miss a curve of two,
And fly right out of its orbit
Into a tailspin screw.

You say it can't be done?
Just watch me, old man.
I got it all planned,
Soon as I get those gloves.

CHAPTER VII - MISCELLANEOUS

And then there are subjects unique to themselves.
They deserve a poem or two.

MY RUBIK'S CUBE

When first I met the Rubik's Cube,
I felt that I was just a rube,
And was afraid I could never solve the cube.

But the cube began to talk to me,
Trying to explain what I couldn't see;
The power that lies within even me.

It said, "Each sequence is a separate key
That helps unlock the mystery
That lies at the very heart of me.

And once you've walked that careful way
That slowly leads to a whole new day,
You'll see each time a brilliant ray.

It's what we find at the very heart
Of everything we take apart,
And that's what makes your fire start."

So I looked around, and now I see
That all things have their mystery,
And what I need are sequences that guarantee
To lead me on and set me free.

I SAW

I saw the mice of yesterday,
And all the rats that ran.
I saw the won'ts that willed to be,
And all the can'ts that can.
I heard the screeching bats at night,
The hissing snakes by day.
I heard the moaning mothers sigh,
The crying children play.

I felt the windmill winds that howl,
The sunset seas that roar.
I felt the soft, sweet empty pain
Of the hopeless, liquored whore.

Without the black there is no white.
Without the night no day.
Without the longing, lonesome loss
No love for which we pray.

A SONG

I heard a song.
He heard it too.
At least I think we heard the same.
But why did mine so linger then,
To him 'twas just a name?

Or is the song inside
Of each and every one that hears?
In some, a thing of beauty
Where sympathies move true.
In others just a pattern
That only passes through.

I CHOOSE

I choose to listen or
    I choose to talk.
I choose to run or
    I choose to walk.
I choose to laugh or
    I choose to wail.
I choose to pass or
    I choose to fail.

My life is not an accident.
It's what my choices make it.
The perfect picture's always there,
But I must stop and take it.

Doing nothing isn't quite
The zero that it seems.
It's just another choice that
Helps to cancel all my dreams.

REDS

Reds
Feds
Meds
Heads
Does it really matter?
When we only see a group
It's just a lot of clatter.

Jim
Tim
Even him
On the other hand is real;
Represents a living soul,
Something we can see and feel.

Classify the birds and fish,
And if you wish
Go grade your lumber.
But grouping of a human soul
Violates a sacred number.

THE INTERSTATE HIGHWAY

The interstate highway stretches mile after mile.
Cars are lined up in a long double file.
Ribbons of concrete cross state after state.
It's the great, grey grid we all seem to hate.

But how would we travel
From coast to coast,
Without the super
Highways we boast?

There was a time
When the trip took ages.
We walked and we rode
Through various stages.

We tried ponies, and stage coaches,
Railroads, and ships.
No matter what,
They were very long trips.

But now, with a semi or bus,
We can travel and carry with us
Anything that we wish to take,
Or any friend that will make
The trip more pleasant and gay,
For the interstate is now the very best way.

RETIREMENT

Thank God I finally made it.
I'll never have to work again.
I can golf on Monday.
Everyday can be a Sunday,
And a nap won't be a sin.

Here I am only sixty-two,
And I'm still as healthy as a horse.
Every day I can decide what I want to do,
And it will be something I enjoy of course.

Six months later I'm still free as a lark.
I do whatever I want from dawn till dark.
But to be perfectly frank, some days aren't so fun.
At day's end I wonder what I've actually done.

I miss my job. I miss its routine.
I even miss the old smelly latrine.
I don't know why but I don't feel so great,
And I can't figure out what it is that I hate.

Surely retirement can be more than this;
A day-to-day feeling of less and less worth.
After six months of seeking the good life
I feel that actually I need a rebirth.

REGRESSION

Why did I drop my spoon on the floor?
Why did I leave my keys in the door?
Why did I miss the red light, and what's more,
Why can't I remember what I last wore?

I seem to be suffering from aging regression.
I'm really not sure in what way,
But I do know that many things I should do
Automatically no longer happen today.

I get up in the morning and put on my shoes,
And I forget how to tie the laces.
Then I look for my teeth and my glasses,
And they seem to be in all the wrong places.

My body is adjusting to aging quite well.
When I go to the fair I can still ring the bell.
But my mind doesn't seem to be doing so well.
What it's going to forget I never can tell.

I guess if I'm going to remember my schedule
I'll have to sit down and make a list.
And I guess I'm going to have to pay attention
If I'm going to stay alive with my mind in a mist.

UP

A slightly different level
Is one of man's more subtle ways
Of indicating to the world
That climbing always pays.

Moving up is always in.
It's almost an obsession.
It saturates our symbolism.
It's used without discretion.

From the snake upon his belly
To the eagle soaring high.
From the weakness of the heel
To the grandeur of the eye.

In fact, for all the Saints and Popes
It would be a bitter cup,
If heaven proved to be straight down
And hell was very up.

WORK

Work is everywhere.
Work is everything.
It may be a melody.
It may be a golden ring.

It may be a ball game.
It may be a classroom test.
It may be an appendectomy.
It may be a happy guest.

It may be a painting.
It may be a field of corn.
It may be a speech.
It may be a tooting horn.

We need to love.
We need to sleep.
We need to laugh.
We need to weep.

But unless we work
We are a lie.
We must work
Or we will die.

CHAPTER VIII - FAMILY

My family has always been the focus of my life.
Consequently, some of my poems are family oriented.

DIVORCE

I loved your mother
So very much.
I was deeply thrilled
By her tender touch.

But slowly time has robbed me
Of the richest thing I had.
I don't know why,
And it's really quite sad.

We drifted apart
Each in a separate boat.
She was never a part of me;
Just more like a friendly coat.

But you, my child,
Are my special part.
I'll love you forever.
You own a piece of my heart.

Oh we'll argue,
And some days we'll fight,
And we'll never resolve
Which one is right.

But we'll keep on loving.
We have no choice.
And because you're my child
I'll forever rejoice.

FAMILY

Mom, Dad, Bro, and Sis,
Smile, Frown, Hug and Kiss,
Grandpa, Grandma, Cousin Sue,
Aunts and Uncles all love you.

Meals, Parties, travel torn,
Weddings, Funerals, Babies born .
Bedtime stories 'til you sleep.
You never have to count the sheep.

Homes are havens from distress,
Whether neat or quite the mess.
Homes protect us from our fears,
Keep us happy through the years.

Families always have a home;
Sometimes large and sometimes small.
It doesn't matter what the size,
If it shelters one and all.

BABYSITTING

We love our grandchildren;
All twenty of them.
We like to see them thrive and grow
For each is a unique gem.

However, we're not their parent.
Parenting we did for their moms and dads.
We're old and we're tired.
And we're no longer in touch with modern fads.

We didn't raise our kids
As they seem to do now.
Times have changed since
Grandma and I spoke our vow.

Therefore, we make poor parents
For our grandchildren in this day.
We're not well equipped
To do it the modern way.

We love to see them, and spoil them,
And send them back to Mom and Dad,
And then sit quietly,
And revel in the pleasure we had.

CHILDREN

You were at the heart
Of my lifetime plan.
You were the ultimate proof
That I was really a man.

And when you arrived
A small bundle of wonder,
I began to realize
You'd tear my life asunder.

Nothing was ever the same
After you and your siblings came
Into my life and made your claim
On every minute and dollar I had to my name.

But I loved you so much
For the joy that you brought,
That nothing on earth
Would I trade for my lot.

And now that you're grown,
And very much on your own,
I'm still very proud
Of the seeds that I've sown.

GRANDFATHERING

I like being a grandfather.
It's an interesting role.
No matter if you're a rich man
Or always on the dole.

Grandkids don't care if you've
Been important or very ordinary.
They only want your attention
To play a game, or to help you carry
Something you're too old to handle,
Or to tell them a story that is scary.

They're more fun to make a deal with,
Than they are to eat a meal with.
They are never rudely curt,
And they're so honest it can hurt.

Though no two of them resemble,
Yet when all of them assemble,
They seem to get along together
No matter what the weather.

I guess I'm very lucky
To have so many sprouts,
And of that I'm now quite certain,
If I ever had some doubts.

MARRIAGE

Marriage is a lifelong game
That only two can play.
No one tries to win this game,
But it's played from day to day.

Some days you're on the same team
Trying to beat a foe.
It may be sickness or may be boredom
When you have no place to go.

Some days you're playing each other
In a fun-filled happy way.
Some days you're angry and can't see
Why your mate won't hear your say.

Some people quit the team,
And try it on their own,
But even if they hate their teammate
It's no fun to play alone.

A long and happy marriage
Is a golden thread we know
Will help us find our way,
No matter where we go.

MY SON

He lives in a Teddy Bear World
Where love is sunshine,
Lack of it is night,
And hate dies of starvation.

It's fun to be the sun,
And have power over the night,
And a little fasting is good for the soul.

PARENTS

God gave us parents
To give us our start.
I know that my parents
Certainly did their part.

When I was a baby
They made sure I was fed.
They burped me. They bathed me.
They provided my bed.

They clothed me
According to the season.
They sacrificed for years
Beyond all human reason.

And then came the day
When I wanted to fly.
They didn't try to stop me.
They didn't even cry.

Now comes the day
When they can't find their way.
They need me and a bib
As I needed them in my crib.

It's not just my duty
To lend them my heart.
I'm proud to help those
Who gave me my start.

FAMILY IS EVERYTHING

Family is the crutch that supports us as we mend our broken spirit.

Family is the water that slakes our most unquenchable thirst.

Family is the sunshine that brightens our cloudiest day.

Family is the food that satisfies our starving soul.

Family is the chorus that produces our sweetest music.

Family is the laughter that puts our problems in perspective.

Family is the everlasting love that surpasses our understanding.

Family is the shawl that keeps our shivering shoulders warm.

Family was there when we entered this world, so very vulnerable.

And Family will be there when we leave this world, Joyfully anticipating the next.

CHAPTER IX – GOD

Some things are so personal that we discuss them only with God.

MY MORNING PRAYER

Good morning God.

I offer up everything I accomplish today to your honor and glory.

I offer up everything I suffer today to the poor souls in purgatory.

I pray that, with the help of thy grace,

I will choose today to run your race.

Forgetting my whim

And running with Him

Who died so that I might live;

Jesus Christ, Your Son,

Who lives and reigns with You and the Holy Spirit,

One God, forever and ever. Amen.

DEATH

When we walk through the Valley of the Shadow of Death
Realizing that heaven's our goal,
And yet knowing we're certainly not ready
To take on such a magnificent role,

I believe we'll find ourselves in a mirror-like place,
Where we're forced by God to come face-to-face
With the kind of person we could have been,
With a great deal more effort, and a great deal less sin.

WHAT AM I?

I love,
And don't know what I do.

I hate,
And don't care who.

I fear,
And don't know why.

I am,
And yet, what am I?

WHY I DO

I do what I can,
And enjoy what I do.
I do what I must,
And might like that too.

I do what I'm told.
I really try to share the load.
I do what I'm asked,
Like an honor's been bestowed.

Because in everything I do,
Even when I sin,
I discover just a little
Of the man within my skin.

ABORTION

Who should decide to set me free?
Oh Lord, I know it should be Thee.
You have planned my destiny.
You know what I was meant to be.
Please don't let them cut me free.
I'm just not ready to be me.

I love my warm and cozy sea
That you expressed for only me.
I want to stay here swimming free
Where I know no harm can come to me.
Don't they know I can't yet see?
Don't they know I'm not yet me?

I need more time if I'm to be
The person I was meant to be.
I need more time in my cozy sea
If I'm to reach my destiny.
Please don't let them cut me free.
I'm just not ready to be me.

Oh no! They've let my lovely sea.
Oh no! They've torn my lifeline free.
Oh no! I will not reach my destiny.
Oh no! There will not ever be a me.

Oh no! I'll not reach my destiny.
Oh No! there will never be a me.

HE'S BEEN SO GOOD TO ME

Oh God has been so good to me.
    That's my reverie.
    That's my ecstasy.
    That's the mystery.
Why has God been so good to me?

NOBODY ELSE

Nobody else needs to know, God.
Nobody but you and me.
Nobody else needs to know
The depth of my misery.

Nobody else needs to know
What it is that we discuss.
Nobody else needs to know
Except us.

DAY IN THE SUN

I've had my day in the sun.
It's been a wonderful run.
I can't say I actually won,
But I've had my day in the sun.

I've had my day in the sun.
Though some days had barely begun,
And I realized I had missed the gun,
But I've still had my day in the sun.

I've had my day in the sun.
When some days I'd carry a ton,
I got help from the Loving One.
I've had my day in the sun.

I've had my day in the sun.
And even though it seems almost done,
I won't complain about my run,
For I've had a glorious day in the sun.

CHAPTER X - LOVE

Love has always been a poetic topic, and so it has been with me.

IN LOVE

Yes I'm in love,
But is it with you?
And I know you're in love,
But dear is it true?

I think we're in love
With love my dear.
We're so young and so full
Of the spring of the year.

Let's share our jokes,
And our lovely long talks.
Let's share the spring
That we find in our walks.

And maybe our love,
If it is love at all,
Will burst into bloom
Sometime in the fall.

LOVE?

I don't hate nobody.
Don't know why I should.
I don't hurt nobody.
Don't know if I could.

I just love my neighbor,
That's just what I do.
Guess that's how God made me,
And that's why I love you.

Everywhere I look I see
The beauty in God's plan.
Don't know why it isn't clear
To every other man.

Guess that I'm just lucky,
Lucky as can be.
And I feel my luckiest
When you say that you love me.

LOVE YOU

Love you?
Of course I do.

Hate you?
Just isn't true.

Spank you?
I have to son.

Love you?
That's the one.

SEX

Sex has been around for a very long time.
Many people actually consider it sublime.
Without it mankind would disappear from the earth.
It's the urge that eventually results in our birth.

But like all things designed to be good,
I'm sure God realized that eventually it would
Be abused, which is something we do
With almost everything, it's true.

He had to create it with lots of pleasure;
Something to lure us during our leisure.
But primarily, He wanted its fate
To be a way of expressing our love for our mate.

Its fruit being children
We would love in return,
But it doesn't look like
We will ever quite learn.

We misuse it.
We abuse it.
We use it for gain.
We abhor it.
We adore it.
We ignore all the pain.

Why can't we respect this great gift from above,
And, in moderation, use it to express our great love?

WISHIN'

Wish that I could tell you
What I really want to say.
Wish that I could make you
Understand it all some way.

Wish that you could guess
The feelin' tearin' at my heart.
Wish that you could comprehend
We're never gonna part.

Wish that I had words to tell you
That your sayin' bye
Ain't gonna change the glimmer
Or the hope that's in my eye.

Wish I had the courage
To explain 'bout you and me;
How I'll never more be happy,
How I never can be free.

Wish that I could make my way
Right back into your heart,
Because I feel my wishin's
Only just begun to start.

WHY?

If I were stars and stars away,
With your love
I'd still be happy.

If I were stripped both in and out,
With your love
I'd still be happy.

If I were sick, both heart and soul,
With your love
I'd still be happy.

Through space and want and suffering too
Your love still makes me happy.

So tell me why, with all your power,
You refuse my pleading cry?
Of all the sins of all the men
Yours would crucify.

WHAT IS LOVE?

Is it an attachment,
A feeling,
Or the ultimate high?
Is it real,
Or is it just a lie?
Does it exist if not shown,
And how does one show it when alone?
By tears,
By laughter,
By hard work,
Or by sacrifice?
Do I love you,
Or just want you?
I love my dog,
And I love my cake,
But is that really love?
Why do I love?
Is it a chemical attraction,
Or is it a physical addiction?
Can a blind person love me?
Do I really love a god I can't see?
Why does a deep love make me fly?
Why does a lost love make me die?

CHAPTER XI - SPECIAL EVENTS

Special events need special words. Frequently, I could not buy a card that said what I wanted to say. Therefore, I wrote some poems.

FIFTY

They're going to say, "You're now over the hill."
That you might as well lie down and quit.
Well, take it from one who has been there my son;
What they're saying is a pile of pure shit.

The truth is you've reached a pinnacle point
Of privilege and power, you will see.
Because now you're the age to joyfully join
The incomparable A.A.R.P.

I'M EIGHTY

Eighty is a lot of years;
A lot of smiles,
And a lot of tears.

Eighty is a long way from
The days when I
Was young and dumb.

Eighty is a lot of miles
I've traveled over bumps,
And trials.

Yet I don't regret
A single day
I've spent in all my work
And play.

I've enjoyed them to my very core,
And here's to maybe eighty more.

ON MY NINETIETH

I've always liked birthday parties.
I like them a lot.
There's ice cream and cake.
And the present I bought.

Everyone's happy
No matter the cost.
No one is bothered
By the year they just lost.

But when you turn ninety
It's a whole different game.
Somehow the party
Doesn't seem quite the same.

You sit there, and you think of the past,
And you wonder how the years could have gone by so fast,

For instance, only yesterday I married this bum,
And he still sticks around like a big wad of gum.
We worked and we traveled all over the place.
It's been like a huge, happy, glorious race.

I wonder how many more years there will be
For me to play euchre and always feel free
To be just this person "You get what you see!"
I've never pretended to be a tall tree.

I guess only God knows the future,
And knowing it for me would be a bad thing.
I'm going to enjoy my ninetieth birthday today,
And not worry about what tomorrow might bring.

HAPPY ONE HUNDREDTH

I couldn't find a card
With a message really neat.
I couldn't write a poem
That was worthy of your feat.

But after sending such a stupid card,
I felt I had to try.
I just hope my clumsy effort
Doesn't make you want to cry.

Of course, I'm saying that I meant well,
But that really won't suffice.
Just be happy that one hundred years
Probably won't come twice.

OUR ANNIVERSARY

The sun is still a shinin',
And the stars are still a twinklin',
And the moon is still a castin'
    Its honey harvest glow.

The world is still a turnin',
And my heart is still a burnin'
With the yearnin' love you kindled
    So very long ago.

MY VALENTINE

I looked for a card,
But none could I find
That came close to saying
What I had on my mind.

When I think of our love,
And all that we've shared;
Only God understood
How well we were paired.

I think of the years;
All the laughter and tears.
I think of the pain
All the sunshine and rain,

All the meals that you've cooked,
All the trips that you've booked,
All the children you bore,
And the grandchildren what's more.

For the life that we've lived
I thank God up above,
And on this Valentine's Day
For the one that I love.

CHAPTER XII - DEMENTIA

I have had three brothers experience dementia before they died. The brother that I was closest to emotionally had to be confined for the last three months he lived. I visited him during that time, and went back home and wrote this poem. I sobbed while I was writing it. If there is anything sadder than dementia I don't know what it is.

DEMENTIA

At first, it was remembering;
Who, what, and where.
Who in the hell did I meet at the store?
She smiled as though she lived right next door.
What was the reason I went up the stair?
Was I looking for something? Why was I there?
Where was I going as I drove down the street?
Was this the corner where we were to meet?

I know my confusion made my life tough,
And bothered my family, and made their life rough.
But why couldn't I just stumble along
For the last few verses left in my song?
Why did they feel compelled, in their own loving way,
To put me in a place where I would just have to stay?

I'm in that place now, and they call it a Home.
Actually it seems much more like a tomb,
With smiling zombies all over the room.
I walk up to one, and I try to say, "Hi."
They smile, and then they just pass me by.

I remember those zombies from the Old Country Store.
We saw them in movies that scared my young core.
We sat on long benches in the warm summer night.
Those movies they showed us were really a sight.

There was Roy Rogers and Trigger;
So good and so brave.
And then came the Zombies
Right out of the grave.

Oh, I have wonderful memories,
And I remember them well,
But nobody listens
As I try to tell
Of the past that I lived.
I won many a race,
But no one understands
In this strange, silent place.

Time seems to have stopped.
All I have is the past.
In this place there's no future.
How long can I last
Where the present's
So empty and vast?

I used to travel a lot.
I no more want to roam.
I only wish
They would let me go home.

ABOUT THE AUTHOR

Fritz Fuhs has been writing for pleasure for more than sixty of his eighty-seven years. He received a Bachelor of Arts degree in English from what used to be called Iowa State Teachers College. He taught English class for three years, and spent the rest of his teaching career as a middle school counselor. He has also published a book on retirement called "Retirement Sucks."

Made in the USA
Monee, IL
02 November 2021

80837400R00069